The Water Cycle

Rebecca Harman

Heinemann Library
Chicago, Illinois

Customer Service 888-454-2279
Visit our website at www.heinemannlibrary.com

Editorial: Melanie Copland
Design: Victoria Bevan and AMR Design
Illustration: Art Construction and
David Woodroffe
Picture Research: Mica Brancic and
Helen Reilly
Production: Duncan Gilbert

Originated by Chroma Graphics (Overseas) Pte. Ltd
Printed and bound in China by CTPS

16 15 14
10 9 8 7 6
ISBN 13 : 9781403470669 (PB)

Library of Congress Cataloging-in-Publication Data

Harman, Rebecca.
    The water cycle / Rebecca Harman.
        p. cm. -- (Earth's processes)
    Includes bibliographical references and index.
    ISBN 1-4034-7059-6 (library binding - hardcover) -- ISBN 978-1-4034-7066-9 (pbk.)
    1. Hydrologic cycle--Juvenile literature. I. Title. II. Series.
    GB848.H37 2005
    551.48--dc22

                                            2005010644

Acknowledgments
The Publisher would like to thank the following for permission to reproduce photographs:
Corbis Sygma/Thomas Dallal **p.18**; Foodpix **p. 21**; UK Meteorological Office/R.K. Pilsbury **p.14 (middle)**; Science Photo Library **p. 13**; 4 (TEK Image), **7**(Tom Van Sant/ Geosphere Project, Santa Monica), **9**(Dr Jeremy Burgess), 12 (Dr Morley Read), **14** (John Howard); Still Pictures/Alan Watson **p.5**, Still Pictures/Ron Giling **p.6**; Still Pictures/Yves Noto Campagnella **p.14 (bottom)**; Still Pictures/Osef Hinterleitner/UNEP **p.15**; Still Pictures/Roland Birke **p.16**; Science Photo Library/Jim Reed **p.17**; Still Pictures/Yann Arthus-Bertrand **p.19**; Still Pictures/Bryan Lynas **p.20**; Science Photo Library **pp.22** (Tony Craddock), 23 (NASA), 24 (Martin Bond), Still Pictures/Jochen Tack **pp. 20, 25**; Still Pictures/Fred Bruemmer **p.26**; Still Pictures/P&A MacDonald/WWI **p.27**; Digital Vision **p.28**.

Cover photograph of ocean waves reproduced with permission of Corbis/ Gunter Marx.

The Publishers would like to thank Nick Lapthorn for his assistance in the preparation of this book.

Every effort has been made to contact copyright holders of any material reproduced in this book. Any omissions will be rectified in subsequent printings if notice is given to the Publisher.

Contents

Why is Water Important? _____ 4

Where is Most of Earth's Water Found? _____ 7

What is the Water Cycle? _____ 9

How Does Water Get into the Air? _____ 11

How Do Clouds Form? _____ 13

What is Precipitation? _____ 15

What Happens to Water When it Reaches the Ground?____ 18

How is Water Stored on Earth? _____ 20

How Does Water Change the Landscape? _____ 22

How Do We Use Water? _____ 26

Conclusion _____ 28

Fact file _____ 29

Glossary _____ 30

More Books to Read _____ 32

Index _____ 32

Words appearing in the text in bold, like this,
are explained in the Glossary.

Why is Water Important?

How much water did you drink today? All living things on Earth need water to survive. Next time you turn on the faucet for a glass of water, think about where the water may have come from. As you will read later in this book, water is always moving around Earth.

Did you know?

When you brushed your teeth this morning, you probably used as much as $1\frac{1}{2}$ gallons (7 liters) of water. This is enough to fill a soft-drink can more than twenty times.

Many people take water for granted. It gushes from the faucet whenever we need it.

Three-quarters of Earth's surface is covered by water. We are surrounded by it—in oceans, **ice sheets**, lakes, **glaciers**, rivers, underground, in living things, and in the air above us.

Water is not always a liquid. It is found on Earth in three forms —as solid ice, liquid water, and an invisible gas in the air, called **water vapor**. Ice forms when water freezes, like the ice cubes in your freezer. Water vapor forms when water heats up.

Did you know?

More than half of your weight is made up of all the water in your body.

Solid ice, liquid water and invisible water vapor are all present in this scene.

Water is always moving, and as it moves it can change from solid ice to liquid water to water vapor gas. Even the water in a puddle is moving. At any one time, some of the liquid water will be escaping into the air as water vapor, and some of the water vapor will be returning to the liquid water in the puddle.

As water moves it changes the shape of Earth's surface and affects our weather. Waves batter the coastline and wear away rocks. Rivers and glaciers carve valleys into the landscape, and water in the air forms clouds and rain.

Here, water is tumbling down a waterfall in Argentina into a mountain river.

Where is Most of Earth's Water Found?

Most of Earth's water is found in the oceans. If you were to look down on Earth from space, you would see that more than two-thirds of Earth is covered by oceans. The land we live on forms only a small part of the Earth's surface.

Did you know?

An amazing 97 percent of Earth's water is found in the oceans.

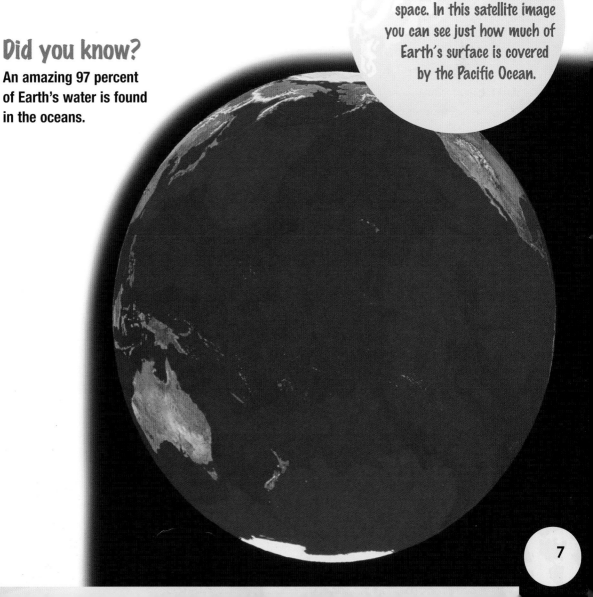

A satellite image is a photograph taken from space. In this satellite image you can see just how much of Earth's surface is covered by the Pacific Ocean.

The oceans transport heat around the world in **ocean currents** that are like giant rivers in the ocean. As the wind blows across the ocean, it drags the surface water with it. This starts the ocean currents moving.

Ocean currents can be warm or cold. Warm currents carry warm water away from the **Equator**, where it is hot, toward the North **Pole** and South Pole, where it is cold. They warm the coastal areas they pass. Cold currents carry cold water away from the poles toward the Equator. They cool down the coastal areas they pass.

The Gulf Stream is a warm ocean current flowing north along the east coast of the United States. It flows across the Atlantic Ocean as the North Atlantic Drift. It then flows north along the west coasts of the British Isles and Norway bringing warm water to these areas. Other areas of the world this far north are very cold, but the warm current helps to keep the west coasts of the British Isles and Norway much warmer than expected.

This is a map of the main ocean currents. Cold currents are shown in blue and warm currents are shown in red.

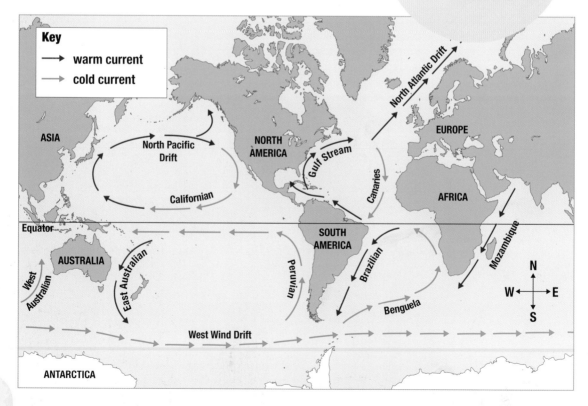

Key
→ warm current
→ cold current

ASIA

North Pacific Drift

Californian

NORTH AMERICA

Gulf Stream

North Atlantic Drift

EUROPE

Canaries

AFRICA

Equator

AUSTRALIA

West Australian

East Australian

Peruvian

SOUTH AMERICA

Brazilian

Benguela

Mozambique

N
W — E
S

West Wind Drift

ANTARCTICA

What is the Water Cycle?

As we use so much water in our daily lives, you may wonder why it never runs out. The reason is that water is always being **recycled**. Water moves around Earth's surface between the air, the land, and the oceans. This is called the **water cycle**.

Warmth from the Sun provides the **energy** for the water cycle. It causes water to escape from the oceans and the surface of Earth into the air as water vapor. This is called **evaporation**. Water vapor rises in the air and cools to form clouds. This is called **condensation**. Clouds can be carried by winds to other areas, where they may produce **precipitation**, such as rain or snow.

Water is always moving around Earth's surface .

If the rain or snow falls into the ocean, the cycle begins again. If rain or snow falls on land, the water begins a long journey back to the ocean. Some water soaks down through the soil to form **groundwater**. Some flows across the surface of Earth in rivers as **surface runoff**. If the water gets trapped anywhere along the way, such as in glaciers or lakes, it is stored there for a period of time. This is called **water storage**. All water eventually makes its way to the ocean to complete the water cycle.

Did you know?

In a 100-year period, a drop of water spends over 97 years in the ocean, a little more than 2 years as ice, about 2 weeks in lakes and rivers, and less than a week in the air.

The water cycle takes place at different speeds in different places. In hot, wet areas near the Equator, such as tropical rain forests, the whole cycle may only take one day. Because it is hot, there is lots of evaporation, resulting in lots of condensation forming clouds and rain. In cold areas, where a lot of water is stored in glaciers and ice sheets, the water cycle may take thousands of years.

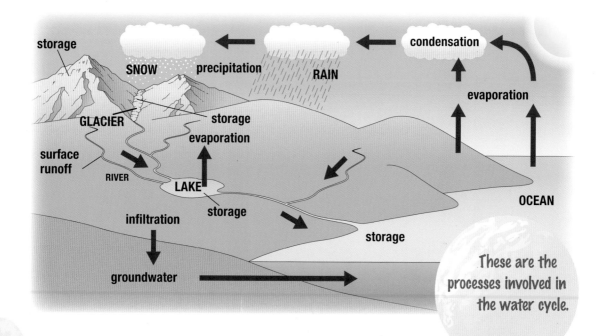

These are the processes involved in the water cycle.

How Does Water Get into the Air?

As the Sun shines, it warms the water on the surface of Earth. The heat from the Sun changes some of this liquid water into an invisible gas called water vapor. This is called evaporation.

Did you know?

You cannot normally see water vapour in the air, but when you boil water the steam that appears is water vapor.

Huge amounts of water evaporate from the oceans, but water also evaporates from the land surface, particularly from lakes, rivers, the soil, and the leaves of plants. You may have wondered how the puddles that form when it rains eventually disappear. They disappear because the water in them evaporates. It escapes into the air as water vapor until there is no liquid water left in the puddle. The ocean is just like a huge puddle. Water is always evaporating from it, but unlike a puddle, the ocean will never dry up. This is because of the water cycle. The water in the ocean is always replaced by rain and river water.

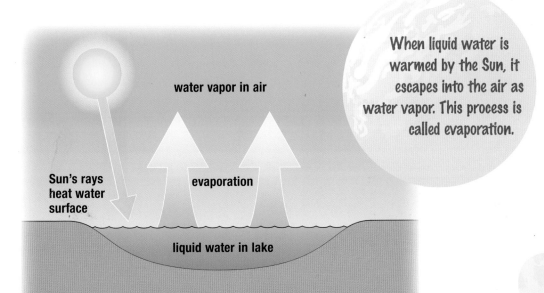

water vapor in air

Sun's rays heat water surface

evaporation

liquid water in lake

When liquid water is warmed by the Sun, it escapes into the air as water vapor. This process is called evaporation.

Evaporation happens faster on a hot day than on a cold day. This is why wet clothes hung out to dry will dry faster on a hot day. The water evaporates from the clothes faster than on a cold day. But even when it is cold, some evaporation takes place, so there is always some water vapor in the air. In the same way, there is much more evaporation in hot areas than in colder areas. In tropical rain forest, a huge amount of water vapor is produced every day, because it is hot.

In the hot, wet tropical rain forest, a huge amount of evaporation occurs every day.

How Do Clouds Form?

When water evaporates the water vapor rises into the air. As it rises it cools because the air gets colder higher up. When the water vapor cools, it changes back into liquid water, in the form of tiny water droplets, to form clouds. This is called condensation. Condensation happens because cold air cannot hold as much water vapor as warm air. You can see condensation happening in your school or home when water vapor in the air condenses into water droplets on a cold window pane.

Clouds form when water vapor condenses in the sky.

The water droplets in the air are so tiny that they do not fall to the ground, but group together to form clouds. If you look at the sky on a cloudy day, you will see that no two clouds are the same. There are many different types of clouds, but they can be grouped into three main types:

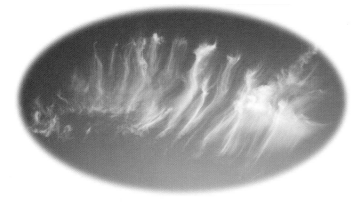

- **Cirrus clouds form high in the air and are thin and wispy.**

- **Stratus clouds form lower in the sky, in sheets or layers. They often cover the Sun and bring rain.**

- **Cumulus clouds are like fluffy cotton balls dotted around the sky.**

Did you know?
Condensation is the opposite of evaporation.

There are three main types of cloud—cirrus (top), stratus (middle) and cumulus (bottom).

What is Precipitation?

Precipitation is any form of solid or liquid water that falls from the air to Earth's surface. It includes rain, snow, sleet, and hail.

Water vapor in the air rises, cools, and condenses to form clouds. The tiny water droplets that make up clouds need to grow larger in order to fall to the ground as rain. They do this by bumping into each other and joining together to make bigger drops. Eventually the drops become so big and heavy that they escape from the cloud and fall to the ground as rain. You may have noticed that not all clouds produce rain. If the droplets do not become heavy enough to fall from the cloud they will stay there, and no rain will fall.

Rain is just one type of precipitation.

Rain is only one of the ways in which the water cycle brings water back to the surface of Earth. Cold clouds are made up of tiny bits of ice, called **ice crystals**. The ice crystals join together, in the same way as water droplets, to form snowflakes. The snowflakes then fall to the ground.

All snowflakes are different. They are made up of tiny ice crystals joined together.

Did you know?

The largest hailstone ever recorded landed in Nebraska in June 2003. It was an amazing 7 inches (17.8 centimeters) across, almost as big as a soccerball!

On the way to the ground, rain and snow may change to form other types of precipitation.

- **Drizzle** is made up of small raindrops.

- **Acid rain** occurs when raindrops combine with **pollution** in the air. This type of rain is harmful, because it kills plants and wears away buildings.

- **Sleet** is made up of melted snowflakes.

- **Hailstones** fall when raindrops freeze and form balls of ice. These range in size from small peas to golf balls. They can be very destructive. In some cases they can break windows, dent cars, and destroy crops.

Hailstones as big as this can cause a lot of damage.

What Happens to Water When it Reaches the Ground?

When rain reaches the land surface, some of it soaks into the ground through small openings in the soil and rocks. This is called **infiltration**. The rest of it flows across the surface as surface runoff.

The amount of water entering the soil or running off across the land surface depends on what that particular land surface is like. In towns and cities, where the ground is covered with streets and concrete buildings, there is very little infiltration. This is because these materials are **impermeable**. This means they do not have spaces to allow water to seep into them. When it rains most of the water flows across the surface as surface runoff until it goes down drains in the gutters. In country areas with fields and bare soil, the infiltration will be much higher because water can get into the spaces in the soil. We say that the soil is **permeable**.

This floodwater is running across the impermeable ground surface in Time Square, New York in 1996.

Once water has entered the soil, it slowly sinks down through the ground until it reaches a layer of impermeable rocks. It collects here to form groundwater. Groundwater flows very slowly through the soil until it eventually reaches rivers or the ocean.

Water moving across the land surface as surface runoff moves downhill in sheets or small channels, called **rills,** until it enters a stream or river. It then continues its journey downhill, joining up with lots of other rivers along the way. Large rivers eventually reach the ocean where they pour out all the water collected along the way, completing the water cycle.

Did you know?

- **Groundwater can take a human lifetime (about 70 years) to travel just over 1 mile (2 kilometers).**

- **Water always moves downhill to the lowest point on Earth's surface, the ocean.**

In Africa, the Tana River in Kenya flows into the Indian Ocean. The water it has collected along the way joins the ocean.

How is Water Stored on Earth?

Within the water cycle, there are several places where water storage takes place. Most water (97 percent) is stored as **salt water** in the oceans. This is where most river water ends up, and it remains there until it evaporates.

Most of Earth's water is stored in the oceans.

Did you know?

When water evaporates from the ocean, the salt is left behind. This means that water vapor in the air is **fresh water**.

Water sometimes gets trapped in ice sheets or glaciers as it makes its journey across Earth's surface toward the ocean. When it gets trapped, it may remain trapped or stored for thousands of years before it is returned to the water cycle when the ice sheet or glacier melts.

Water stored in a glacier can remain there for thousands of years before it rejoins the water cycle.

Small amounts of water are stored as groundwater and in lakes and rivers. Only a tiny amount is stored in the **atmosphere** as water vapor. Water vapor is very important, because it is involved in all Earth's weather, such as the formation of clouds, rain, snow, hail, and fog.

Can you think of other places where water is stored?

How Does Water Change the Landscape?

Water plays a very important role in shaping Earth's surface. Flowing water has the power to pick up and carry away soil and rock in a process called **erosion**.

This V-shaped valley is part of the Grand Canyon in northern Arizona. It was created by the power of the river cutting down into the rocks.

How does water cause soil erosion?

Water flowing over the surface of the land, in sheets or rills, can cause huge amounts of soil erosion. The water removes the top layer of the soil and carries it away. The amount of erosion increases if the soil is bare and loose.

How do rivers change the landscape?

Rivers begin high in the mountains. Over thousands of years, they cut deep, V-shaped valleys into the land. These can form spectacular scenery, such as in the Yellowstone Park in Wyoming.

Fast-flowing rivers can be cloudy with huge amounts of **sediment** from soil and rock erosion. The power of the water carries this sediment downstream, eroding the sides of the river as it does so.

As rivers approach the ocean, they get wider and deeper. They carve out much wider valleys as the river bends from side to side across the valley floor. Sometimes a river will flood over its banks and out onto the valley floor. As it does so, it dumps the sediment it is carrying in a process called **deposition**. This creates a wide, flat valley floor, called a floodplain.

When a river finally reaches the ocean, it deposits any remaining sediment it is carrying, sometimes forming a huge, fan-shaped pile of mud, called a **delta**.

This is the Mississippi River delta in Louisiana. The sediment has been deposited in many huge fan shapes.

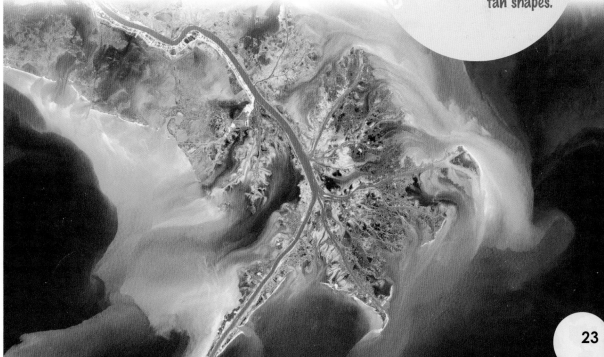

How do glaciers change the landscape?

Glaciers are very slow-moving rivers of ice. They form when snow collects high in the mountains and hardens to form ice. They are found in cold countries, such as Greenland and Iceland, and high in the mountains in Alaska and in the Alps in Europe.

As they move, glaciers carve out wide, deep U-shaped valleys, called glacial troughs. They sharpen mountains into narrow ridges and pinnacles, called **arêtes** and **horns**.

The water stored as ice in glaciers eventually reaches the ocean when it melts, but this may take thousands of years.

Garschen valley in Switzerland is an example of a wide U-shaped valley formed by the passage of a glacier.

How do oceans change the landscape?

Waves have enormous destructive power and can create very dramatic landforms. Waves crashing into a cliff face will gradually erode it at the bottom until the overhanging rock above falls down. Areas of soft rock will be eroded quickly to form bays. Areas of harder rock will erode more slowly and form **headlands**, caves, arches, and **stacks**.

Waves can cause dramatic landforms, such as this arch found on the island of Gozo, near Malta.

How Do We Use Water?

We use water in many different ways. We use it for transportation, sports, and leisure. In the home we use clean water for drinking, cooking, and washing. In factories water is used to cool and clean machinery. Farmers use huge amounts of water for their animals and crops. Some use large sprinkler systems to **irrigate** the land.

Water is stored for human use in lakes, called **reservoirs**. It can be pumped through pipes from reservoirs to homes, schools, shops, factories, or wherever it is needed. Reservoirs are created along rivers by building **dams**. The dam traps the water behind it, forming a reservoir, but it also upsets the natural balance of the river. When the dam is created, a large area of land is flooded to form the reservoir. Anyone living in this area has to move out. The dam also traps a large amount of sediment that would otherwise travel down the river. Over time this leads to the reservoir filling up with sediment, so less water can be stored.

This huge sprinkler system in California provides water to help crops grow. All around is dry desert.

We take water for granted. We simply have to turn on a faucet, and clean, safe water comes out. However in some countries, such as in central Africa, this is not the case. People may have to walk for hours to collect water from wells and then carry it back to their homes.

Did you know?

In the United States each person uses around 132 gallons (600 liters) of water per day. In Nigeria, like many other developing countries, each person uses just 20 gallons (90 liters) per day.

The way we use water can have serious effects on the environment and on future supplies of water. In many places so much water is being used that some rivers and reservoirs are in danger of drying up.

This reservoir in Jura, France has been created by building a dam.

Conclusion

More than two-thirds of Earth's surface is covered by water. Water is continually moving around the Earth's surface, circulating between the air, the land, and the oceans in the water cycle.

In the water cycle, water evaporates from the surface of Earth, then rises, cools, and condenses to form clouds and precipitation.
If the precipitation falls into the ocean, the cycle begins again. If it falls on land, it begins a long journey back to the ocean, traveling as groundwater or surface runoff, or in rivers. If the water gets trapped anywhere along the way, it may be stored for some time. All water eventually makes its way to the ocean to complete the water cycle.

As it moves around, water plays a very important role in shaping the surface of Earth and affecting our weather.

We use water in many different ways, mainly at home, in industry, and for farming. The way we use water can have serious effects on the environment and future supplies of water.

This iceberg is floating in the sea.

Fact File

How much water do we use in one day?

Activity	Amount of water used	
Taking a bath	11–22 gallons	(50–100 liters)
Taking a shower	9 gallons	(40 liters)
Watering the lawn	154 gallons	(700 liters)
Dish washing	11–44 gallons	(50–200 liters)
Clothes washing	22 gallons	(100 liters)
Toilet flushing	$3\frac{1}{2}$–$5\frac{1}{2}$ gallons	(15–25 liters)
Brushing your teeth	$1\frac{1}{2}$ gallons	(7 liters)
Drinking water	$\frac{1}{2}$ gallon	(2 liters)

Where is Earth's water found?

Location	Amount (percentage)
Oceans	97
Ice sheets and glaciers	2
Lakes, rivers, and the air	1

Did you know?

People all over the world drink about 20 billion gallons (89 billion liters) of bottled water every year. About 3 billion gallons (13 billion liters) are drunk by Americans alone.

Glossary

acid rain rain water that has been polluted by acid in the air. It kills plants and wears away buildings

arête narrow ridge formed by a glacier in mountainous regions

atmosphere blanket of air that surrounds Earth

condensation when water vapor changes into liquid water

dam barrier built across a river to hold back water and create a reservoir

delta fan-shaped area of sediment formed where a river meets the ocean or a lake

energy power that is used to make something

Equator imaginary line that circles the middle of Earth

erosion wearing down and removal of sediment

evaporation when liquid water changes into water vapor (a gas)

fresh water water that is not salty. Lakes, ponds, and rivers are fresh water

glacier slow-moving river of ice

groundwater water flowing very slowly underground

headland piece of land that sticks out into the sea

horn sharp peak formed by a glacier in mountainous regions

iceberg huge chunk of floating ice

ice crystal tiny piece of ice in a cloud

ice sheet thick layer of ice covering a large area, such as Antarctica

impermeable does not have spaces to allow water to seep through (example: concrete)

infiltration rain soaking into the ground through small openings in the soil and rocks

irrigate supply land with water so that crops can grow

ocean current flow of water in an ocean caused by winds blowing the surface of the water

permeable has spaces that allow water to seep through (example: soil)

Pole very cold region at the North and South ends of Earth

pollution things that are harmful to the environment (example: car exhaust fumes)

precipitation rain, sleet, snow, or hail

recycle reuse

reservoir lake used for storing water

rill small channel in the ground surface where water flows

salt water water that contains salt. The water in the oceans is salt water

satellite image photograph taken from space

sediment bits of rock and mud

stack column of eroded rock in the ocean near the coast

surface runoff water flowing across the surface of Earth in rivers

tributary side river that joins a main river

water cycle the movement of water around Earth's surface, between the air, the land, and the oceans

water storage place where water is trapped or stored for a time. This could be in a lake or glacier

water vapor water in the air in the form of an invisible gas

More books to read

Graham, Ian. *Earth's Precious Resources: Water.* Chicago: Heinemann Library, 2004.

Pipe, Jim. *Earthwise: Water.* London: Franklin Watts, 2004.

Royston, Angela. *The Lives and Times of a Drop of Water.* Chicago: Raintree, 2005.

Index

acid rain 17
arches 25
arêtes 24
atmosphere 21

body, water in the 5
bottled water 21, 29

clouds 6, 9, 10, 13, 14, 15, 16, 21, 28
   cirrus clouds 14
   cumulus clouds 14
   stratus clouds 14
condensation 9, 10, 13, 28
currents 8

dams 26, 27
deltas 23
deposition 23
drizzle 17

energy 9
erosion 22, 23, 25
evaporation 9, 10, 11–12, 20, 28

fog 21
fresh water 20

glacial troughs 24
glaciers 5, 6, 10, 20, 21, 24, 29
groundwater 10, 19, 21, 28
Gulf Stream 8

hail, hailstones 15, 16, 17, 21
horns 24

ice 5, 6, 10, 24
ice crystals 16
ice sheets 5, 10, 20, 21, 29

impermeable materials 18, 19
infiltration 18
irrigation 26

lakes 5, 10, 29
landforms 22–25

oceans 5, 7–8, 10, 11, 19, 20, 29

permeable materials 18
pollution 17
precipitation 9, 15–17, 28

rain 6, 9, 10, 15, 17, 18, 21
recycling 9
reservoirs 26, 27
rills 19, 22
rivers 5, 6, 19, 23, 27, 29

salt water 20
sediment 23, 26
sleet 15, 17
snow, snowflakes 9, 10, 15, 16, 17, 21, 24
surface runoff 10, 18, 19, 28

valleys 22, 23, 24

water cycles 9–10, 11, 20, 28
water storage 10, 20–21
water usage 4, 26–27, 28, 29
water vapor 5, 6, 9, 11, 12, 13, 15, 20, 21
wells 27